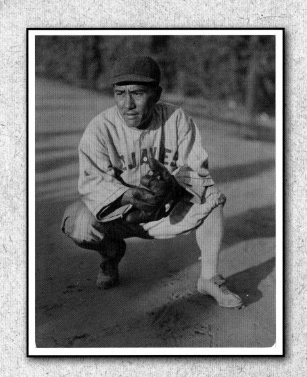

TO HOWARD REEVES, EDITOR EXTRAORDINAIRE
— MM

TO MY PARENTS AND MY SISTER JUNE, AND MY
"AMERICAN FAMILY," KATIE YAMASAKI, WITHOUT
WHOM IT WOULD HAVE BEEN IMPOSSIBLE TO
COMPLETE THIS PROJECT
— YS

ZENI WATCHED THE WOODEN BAT THWACK THE BASEBALL, hurling it high and straight. He was eight years old, and it was the first time he'd seen a baseball game, but he was hooked.

"Father, I want to play!" he told his dad.

"You're too small," his father said.

"Too frail," added his mother.

But Zeni didn't listen. He *had* to play.

The other kids laughed at him.

"Zeni, you're a mouse!" one boy hooted.

"A teeny tiny one!" another kid called.

None of it mattered. When Zeni had a ball or bat in his hand, he felt like a giant. And soon he played like one.

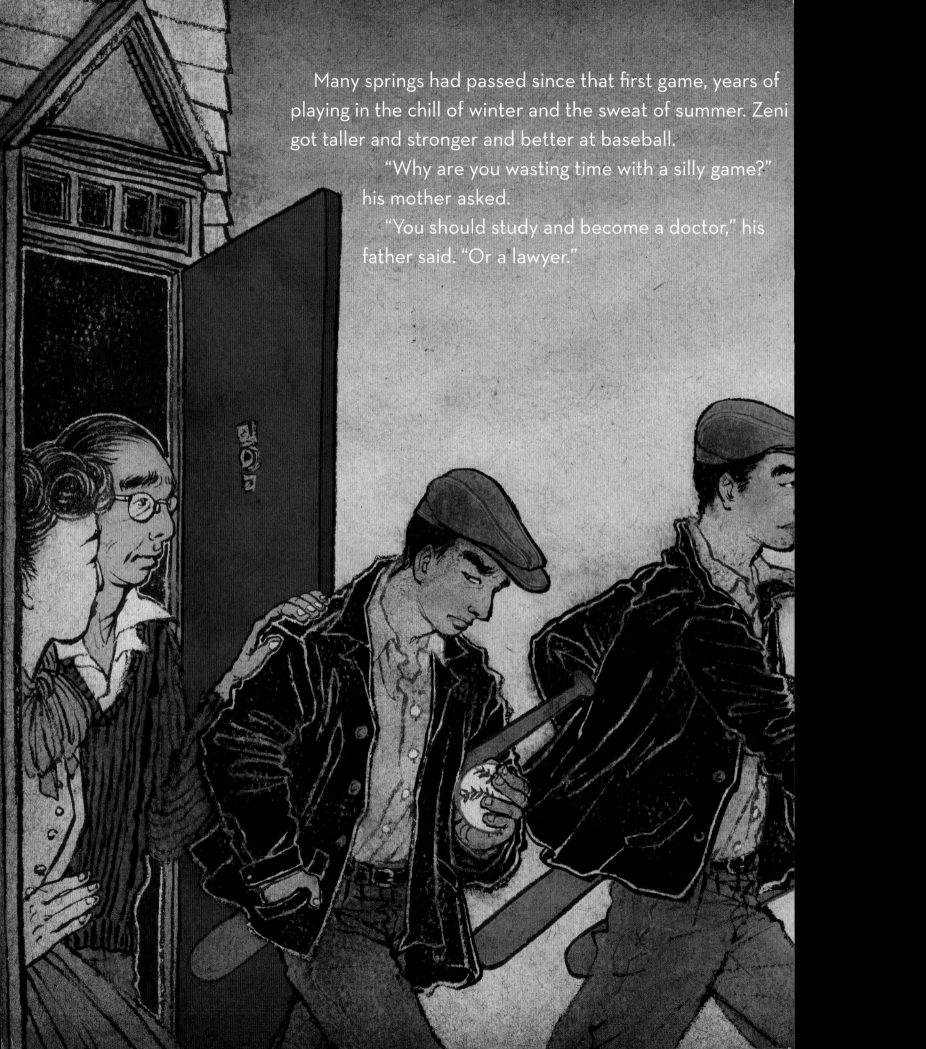

Many springs had passed since that first game, years of playing in the chill of winter and the sweat of summer. Zeni got taller and stronger and better at baseball.

"Why are you wasting time with a silly game?" his mother asked.

"You should study and become a doctor," his father said. "Or a lawyer."

But Zeni knew exactly what he wanted to do, and when he grew up, he coached, managed, and played baseball in the Fresno Nisei League and the Fresno Twilight League. He was barely five feet tall and weighed only one hundred pounds, but he was a star player, casting a big shadow in baseball.

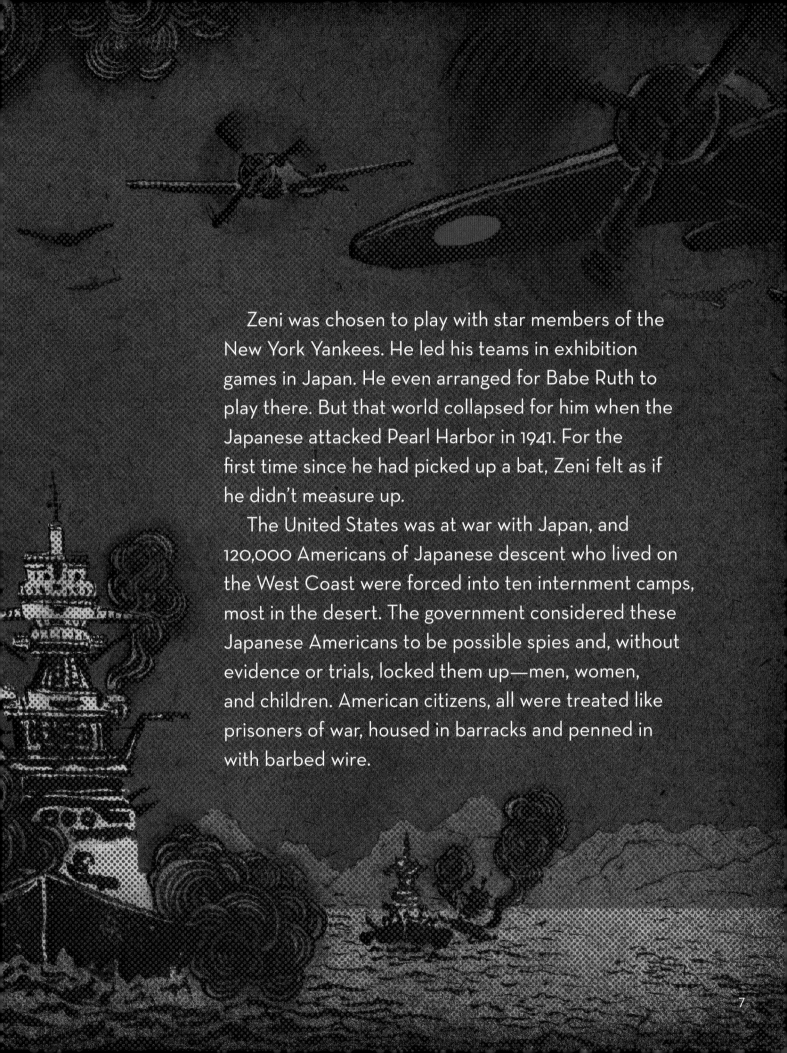

Zeni was chosen to play with star members of the New York Yankees. He led his teams in exhibition games in Japan. He even arranged for Babe Ruth to play there. But that world collapsed for him when the Japanese attacked Pearl Harbor in 1941. For the first time since he had picked up a bat, Zeni felt as if he didn't measure up.

The United States was at war with Japan, and 120,000 Americans of Japanese descent who lived on the West Coast were forced into ten internment camps, most in the desert. The government considered these Japanese Americans to be possible spies and, without evidence or trials, locked them up—men, women, and children. American citizens, all were treated like prisoners of war, housed in barracks and penned in with barbed wire.

ZENI, HIS WIFE, AND THEIR TWO TEENAGE SONS WERE SENT TO A CAMP in Gila River, Arizona. Outside, the camp was bleak and gray and dusty. Inside, the barracks were stark, with crowded rows of cots and not much else. Families bustled around, trying to make a home out of nothing, hanging up curtains, arranging tea sets on footlockers, piling dolls and stuffed animals on cots.

Zeni stood staring at the dry earth, which was broken up every now and then by a few scrubby bits of green. In all the brown and gray, with a dull, coppery sky overhead, he felt as if he were shrinking into a tiny hard ball.

There was only one thing that could make the desert camp a home—baseball. Zeni unpacked his favorite photo, the one that showed him in uniform, lined up with baseball legends Babe Ruth and Lou Gehrig towering like redwood trees beside him. He had played with the Yankee stars in an exhibition game back home in Fresno, and he hadn't felt small at all. He pinned the picture up over his bed. He was going to play baseball again. Here, in the desolate

First he would need a playing field. There was plenty of empty space, but it was dotted with sagebrush and clotted with rocks. It didn't look like much of a field.

Zeni started by chopping down the plants and digging up the rocks, spending long hours in the blazing sun.

"What are you doing, Dad?" his son Howard asked.

"Can't play baseball without a field," Zeni grunted.

"We're going to play baseball?" Howard grinned and started picking up rocks, too.

Soon Howard's brother, Harvey, joined them. Then other boys and men drifted to where Zeni and his sons were bent over in the glaring heat. By the end of the day, dozens of people were working on the field, not planting a crop but unplanting, making the ground a smooth surface.

Once the brush and the biggest rocks had been cleared, Howard and Harvey were ready to set up the bases.

"Looks good," Howard said. "We're almost set."

Zeni shook his head. "Nowhere close. We're making a real ballpark, and we'll do it right." He walked over to the camp commander's office. Ten minutes later, he emerged into the bright sun, smiling.

"We've got it!" He clapped his hands.

"What?" asked Howard. "What have we got?"

"A bulldozer to level the field," Zeni replied. "The commander said we can borrow the camp's."

As Zeni drove the bulldozer, crowds gathered to watch.

"What's he doing?" an old woman asked her grandson.

"He's making a baseball field," the young man answered.

"A baseball field? Whatever for?" she asked.

Her son smiled. "So we can play."

Once the ground had been smoothed, Harvey brought out his bat and ball. "Now we can play, right?" he asked.

Zeni shook his head. He still wasn't satisfied. The wind kicked up so much dust from the dry soil that the players would be eating dirt.

"We have to do this right." He looked around the camp, hoping to find something to solve the dust problem. Then he got an idea. He diverted an irrigation line to the field and flooded it with water. Once the heat had dried the ground, the dirt was baked into clay—a clean, hard surface without all the dust.

"Now, Dad?" asked Howard, tossing a ball between his hands. "It looks great!"

"Almost," Zeni answered. "But we're not there yet."

17

The irrigation line gave Zeni another idea. He laid pipe from the laundry room to the field and planted grass in the infield and quick-growing castor beans along the edge of the outfield. The pipe fed water to the plants, and soon the clay and grass took on the shape of a baseball field with a castor bean fence. Zeni smiled. Now it was beginning to look real.

"Come on, Dad," Howard urged. "Can't we at least mark the bases now?"

"Go ahead," Zeni agreed. "But we're not done yet."

Howard used flour to chalk the foul lines, and his mom sewed the bases from rice sacks.

"It's perfect!" Harvey said.

"What about the spectators, the fans?" Zeni asked. "Where will they go?"

Both boys shrugged. "Can't they just stand around?" Howard asked.

"Or we can build rows of bleachers," Zeni said. "Like on a real baseball field."

That night Zeni and his sons snuck out of their barracks. They were not allowed outside after dark. Zeni felt like a boy again, tiptoeing out of the house with his bat and glove so his parents wouldn't see him.

A guard's light swept across the yard, and Zeni motioned to the boys to flatten themselves against the barracks. They waited for the beam to pass, then crept on. They didn't know that the guard had seen them but the commander had told him to let them go, so long as they didn't escape. The commander was curious to see what Zeni wanted now.

The three of them scrounged wood from the fence surrounding the camp. They removed every other post, careful not to damage the fencing. Then they took wood from the camp lumberyard. That gave them enough material to build a backstop and five rows of bleachers behind it.

The next day they set to work again, this time sawing wood and nailing boards. When Howard finished hammering the last row of seats, he wiped the sweat from his forehead and gaped at what they had made. There, in the middle of the desert, on the edge of an internment camp, was an official-looking baseball field. The rest of the place slumped, dreary and sad, but the baseball field glowed green with hope.

"Now, Dad?" Harvey asked.

"Almost." Zeni smiled. "We have the field. Now we need the equipment."

He passed a hat among the families, collecting money for gear. In an hour he had enough to send for bats, balls, mitts, and hats from Holman's Sporting Goods back home in Fresno. Several women sewed uniforms out of potato sacks.

When the box of equipment arrived, Zeni let Howard open it. "Now, Howard," he said. "Now we can play ball!"

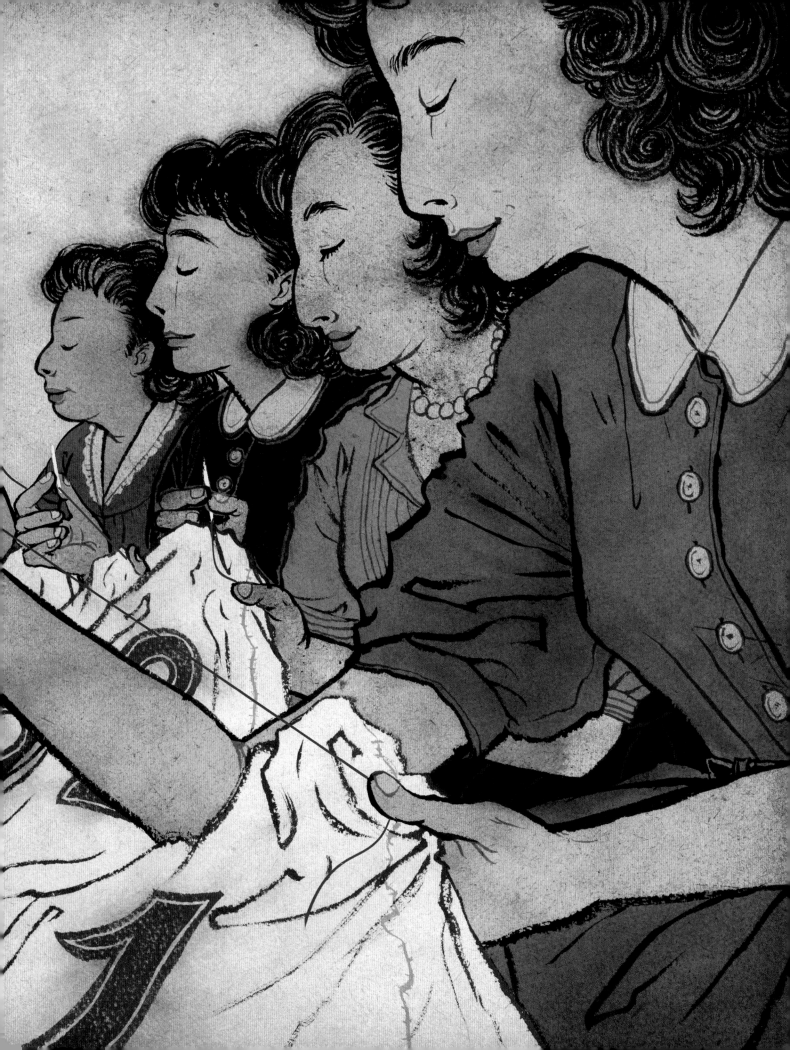

THAT FIRST GAME, ON A BRIGHT MAY DAY, HALF THE CAMP TURNED out to watch the teams that Zeni had organized. A breeze stirred the new grass. The sun bathed everything in a gentle warmth. It was a perfect day for a baseball game. Six thousand people filled the bleachers and spilled onto the scrubby ground behind them and along the sides of the stands.

Zeni leaned over home plate, the bat held firmly in his hands. He looked at Howard, already on first base; at Harvey, now on second; at the neat white lines marking the field. His eyes scanned the bleachers filled with cheering fans. He watched the pitcher cradling the ball, pulling back his arm, getting ready to throw.

Zeni focused on the blur of white as it zoomed closer. The weight of the bat felt so familiar and natural, it was like a part of his body. He waited until just the right moment . . .

Whack. The bat met the ball with a crisp, splintering sound. Zeni threw the bat down and ran. He ran to first base, then second, then third, his eyes following the arc of the ball as it soared up and away, far over the barbed wire fence.

Howard and Harvey jogged to home plate before him, arms raised, grins plastered on their faces. "Now!" they yelled. "Now!"

"Now!" Zeni shouted back. He knew he was still behind a barbed wire fence, but he felt completely free, as airy and light as the ball he had sent flying.

Right now there was nothing else he wanted to do. Just this, right now, right here. It didn't matter whether his team won or lost. Like the powerful champion he was, he felt he could touch the sky if he wanted. "Now!" he roared as he crossed home plate.

He felt ten feet tall, playing the game he loved so much. Nothing would ever make him feel small again.

AFTERWORD

KENICHI ZENIMURA (January 25, 1900–November 13, 1968) was known as the "Dean of the Diamond," the father of Japanese American baseball. As a player, he excelled at all nine positions. As a coach and manager, he led his teams to victory after victory. Born in Japan, Zeni moved to Hawaii with his family when he was eight. There he discovered the game that would shape his life. He played baseball throughout school and continued playing after he graduated and moved to Fresno, California.

Zeni threw right-handed and batted left-handed. Date of photo unknown.

He founded the Fresno Athletic Club and won the Japanese American state championship three years in a row. He went on to tour in Japan, popularizing the sport in his native country. When the Yankees came to Fresno to play an exhibition game in October 1927, four Japanese American players were picked for their teams, Zeni among them.

Then Pearl Harbor was bombed in 1941, and President Franklin Roosevelt signed Executive Order 9066, authorizing the internment of all people of Japanese ancestry living on the West Coast (the coast seen as most vulnerable, being nearest to Japan and its powerful naval forces). Although they were loyal American citizens, they were considered dangerous, possible spies for Japan. Zeni and his family were sent to one of the ten camps—the Gila River War Relocation Center in Arizona. Like the other camps, the center was fenced with barbed wire. Although it was later removed at the Gila camp, the barbed wire was illustrated in this book to stress that this was a prison to the people there.

Despite the harsh conditions, Zeni kept playing baseball, building a field out of nothing. He organized thirty-two teams into three divisions, games were scheduled every day. When the camp closed in November 1945, the field was left to the desert creatures. Back home in Fresno, Zeni built a new ball field.

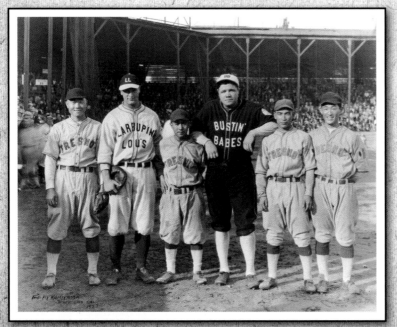

Zeni is between Lou Gehrig (left) and Babe Ruth at an exhibition game in Fresno, California, 1927.

After their experience playing ball in the internment camp, both of Zeni's sons went on to play big-league baseball in Japan for the Hiroshima Carp.

In July 2006, Kenichi Zenimura was posthumously inducted into the Shrine of the Eternals, the national equivalent of the Baseball Hall of Fame in Cooperstown, New York, but whose election of individuals is based on merits other than just statistics and playing ability. His son Kenso Howard Zenimura accepted the award on his father's behalf.

AUTHOR'S NOTE

I first came across Kenichi Zenimura when I was doing research on the Japanese internment camps of World War II. I was deeply impressed by photographs of the baseball field he so lovingly crafted in the middle of the desert. It was a symbol of hope, of the resilience of the human spirit, of making life normal in the most abnormal times. The other photo that struck me was that of Zeni in his baseball uniform flanked by Lou Gehrig and Babe Ruth, the ultimate all-American heroes. Those images act as bookends to this story about the great American pastime and the role it plays in our lives—so much more than a mere sport. Sometimes, in the right place at the right time and in the right hands, baseball can make dreams come true.

ARTIST'S NOTE

When Abrams asked me to illustrate this book, I thought it was my duty, as a recent transplant from Japan, to visualize this story of one Japanese American man's dreams and courage during the war between the United States and my home country. The story has powerful messages, such as the importance of

Zeni (left) and his son Howard on Zenimura Field at Gila River War Relocation Center in Arizona, c. 1942—45

striving to be our best even during the toughest of times, and reminds us that we are all Americans regardless of where our ancestors are from.

My studio mate Katie Yamasaki is a children's book author. Her father's family was imprisoned in the American internment camps, and she has given me a better understanding of the subject. While I was working on *Barbed Wire Baseball*, Katie was also working on a book based on her family's experiences called *Fish for Jimmy*.

My job as an artist is to have you travel through Zeni's experiences in the most detailed and accurate way possible. Unfortunately, almost no visual references of Zeni during his camp days are available. Zeni's likeness was based on a couple of photos I found of him before he entered the camp. Camp references were based on intensive Internet research. Some photographs I used were taken at the Gila River War Relocation Center, but I also used photographs from other camps.

References for one of the most important symbols of hope, the teams' uniforms, unfortunately could not be found. After extensive searching and correspondence with the editor, we decided to use a handmade baseball uniform from the same period, which I had seen at the exhibition Sporting Life at the Fashion Institute of Technology, as a basic pattern. I then added a generic color and look to them.

BIBLIOGRAPHY

AUTHOR

PERIODICALS

Davis, David. "A Field in the Desert That Felt Like Home: An Unlikely Hero Sustained Hope for Japanese-Americans Interned in World War II." *Sports Illustrated*, November 16, 1998.

"The Dean of Japanese American Baseball." *Asian Sun News* 12, no. 4 (August 15, 2005): 5.

Mineta, Norman, as told to Susan Schindehette. "The Wounds of War: A California Congressman Recalls the Trauma of World War II Internment." *People Weekly* 28, no. 4 (December 14, 1987).

Rhoden, William C. "Baseball's Japanese Roots Survive Test of Time and Will." *New York Times*, June 23, 2007.

WEB SITES

Baseball-Reference.com. Kenichi Zenimura biographical information. Last modified September 3, 2011. http://www.baseball-reference.com/bullpen/Kenichi_Zenimura

Ellsesser, Stephen. "Zenimura a True Baseball Ambassador." May 10, 2007. MLB.com. http://mlb.mlb.com

Nisei Baseball Research Project. "Help Nominate Kenichi Zenimura for the Buck O'Neil Lifetime Achievement Award." July 1, 2010. http://www.niseibaseball.com/Nominate_Zenimura_for_the_Buck_ONeil_Award.html

"Kenichi Zenimura: The Dean of Japanese American Baseball." http://www.niseibaseball.com/html%20articles/Nisei%20Legends/zenimura.htm

MULTIMEDIA

Diamonds in the Rough: Zeni and the Legacy of Japanese-American Baseball. Great American Sports Stories Series. Derry, NH: Chip Taylor Communications, 1999. DVD.

Public Radio International. *Baseball Behind Barbed Wire*. Audio slide show. http://www.pri.org/pri-videos/baseball-behind-barbedwire.html.

ARTIST

BOOKS

Daniels, Roger, Sandra C. Taylor, and Harry H. L. Kitano. *Japanese Americans From Relocation to Redress*. Revised Edition. Seattle: University of Washington Press, 1986, 1991.

Gall, John, and Gary Engel. *Sayonara Home Run!: The Art of the Japanese Baseball Card*. San Francisco: Chronicle Books, 2006.

Peary, Danny, and Mary Tiegreen. *1,001 Reasons to Love Baseball*. New York: Stewart, Tabori & Chang, 2004.

Quigley, Martin. *The Crooked Pitch: The Curveball in American Baseball History*. New York: Algonquin, 1984.

Stanley, Jerry. *I Am an American: A True Story of Japanese Internment*. New York: Crown, 1996.

WEB SITES

AntiqueAthlete.com. http://www.antiqueathlete.com.

Dave's Vintage Baseball Cards. https://www.gfg.com/baseball/nuaquire.shtm

"Japanese-American Internment Camps." http://www.bookmice.net/darkchilde/japan/camp.html.

Masumi Hayashi Photography. "Gila River Relocation Camp." http://www.masumihayashi.com/html/gila.html.

Nisei Baseball Research Project. "Kenichi Zenimura: The Dean of Japanese American Baseball." http://www.niseibaseball.com/html%20articles/Nisei%20Legends/zenimura.htm

Smithsonian American Art Museum and Renwick Gallery. "The Art of Gaman: Arts and Crafts from the Japanese American Internment Camps, 1942–1946." http://americanart.si.edu/exhibitions/archive/2010/gaman.

MULTIMEDIA

American Pastime. Directed by Desmond Nakano. Burbank, CA: Warner Home Video, 2007. DVD.

Diamonds in the Rough: Zeni and the Legacy of Japanese-American Baseball. Great American Sports Stories Series. Derry, NH: Chip Taylor Communications, 1999. DVD.

INDEX

The illustrations in this book were made with Japanese calligraphy brush and ink on TH Saunders Waterford paper, then scanned and colored entirely in Adobe Photoshop 3 and 5.5.

The Library of Congress has catalogued the hardcover edition of this book as follows:

Moss, Marissa.
  Barbed wire baseball / by Marissa Moss; illustrated by Yuko Shimizu.
    p. cm.
  ISBN 978-1-4197-0521-2
1. Baseball—United States—History—20th century—Juvenile literature. 2. Japanese Americans—Evacuation and relocation, 1942-1945—Juvenile literature. 3. World War, 1939-1945—Juvenile literature. I. Shimizu, Yuko, 1965– ill. II. Title.
GV863.A1M676 2013
2012010021

ISBN for this edition: 978-1-4197-2058-1

Printed and bound in China
10 9 8 7 6 5 4 3

Abrams Books for Young Readers are available at special discounts when purchased in quantity for premiums and promotions as well as fundraising or educational use. Special editions can also be created to specification. For details, contact specialsales@abramsbooks.com or the address below.

ABRAMS The Art of Books
195 Broadway, New York, NY 10007
abramsbooks.com